T0037835

To all those whose lives appear to be broken or shattered . . .
there is so much beauty when you embrace the pieces and glue them all together.—S. B. K.

Y para Amparo, tu amistad es un tesoro y tu creatividad me inspira.—S. B. K.

SUSAN B. KATZ is an award-winning, bestselling, Spanish author, National Board-Certified teacher, and keynote speaker. She has written more than twenty books, including *The Story of Ruth Bader Ginsburg, The Story of Frida Kahlo,* and *Meditation Station,* which won the 2020 International Book Award for Best Mind/Body/Spirit Children's Book. She lives near San Francisco, California. Find out more about her at SusanKatzBooks.com.

LINDA SCHWALBE studied illustration at the Burg Giebichenstein University of Art and Design Halle and at the Berlin University of the Arts. Inspired by discoveries and adventures, music and nature, she is happiest painting with acrylics. She is the author/illustrator of *Ida and the World Beyond the Kaiserzipf* and winner of the prestigious Serafina Award for the most promising new illustrator in Germany. This is Linda Schwalbe's second book for NorthSouth. She lives and works in Leipzig, Germany.

GAUDÍ

Architect of Imagination

Susan B. Katz · Linda Schwalbe

North
South

Antoni Gaudí's father, grandfather, great-grandfather, and great-great-grandfather all worked as metalsmiths, bending and shaping copper into place. It seemed like magic to Antoni. He looked down at his sore legs. If only these artisans could use their metalsmith magic to make his legs feel better. Antoni had an illness that made it hard for him to walk.

He did not attend school because he could not sit for very long. Antoni, a blond-haired, blue-eyed Spaniard with wobbly legs, felt different from everyone else.

His four brothers and sisters, and all the neighborhood children, went off to school. But Antoni would stay home and wander his family's ranch for hours on end, going on nature adventures. Since walking was a challenge, he traveled by donkey wherever he went. As six-year-old Antoni rode slowly around the land surrounding his family's home in Reus, Spain, he absorbed all the shapes, sights, and sounds of the land.

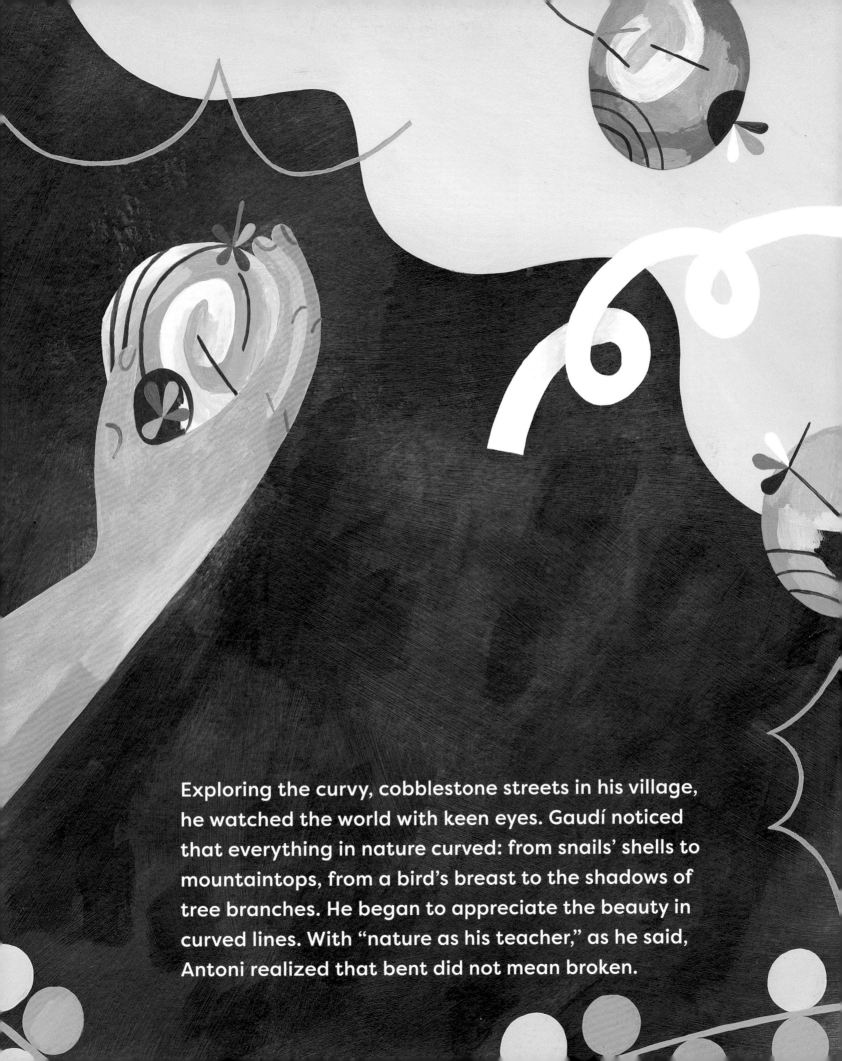

Exploring the curvy, cobblestone streets in his village, he watched the world with keen eyes. Gaudí noticed that everything in nature curved: from snails' shells to mountaintops, from a bird's breast to the shadows of tree branches. He began to appreciate the beauty in curved lines. With "nature as his teacher," as he said, Antoni realized that bent did not mean broken.

By age sixteen, Antoni's pain had subsided enough that he could attend the university. Gaudí moved to Barcelona from the countryside. He wanted to draw and recreate undulated ocean waves, snail's shells, and the jagged tree branches that he had seen as a child.

But Antoni did not want to work in metal. He was fascinated with ceramic tile and stone, earth rather than fire. There, among a sea of artists and architects, he learned to design and construct buildings from some of the greatest artists in all of Europe.

Fascinated with the crooked line, Gaudí produced entire
homes and rooftops that were curved. He said, "The straight
line belongs to man, but the curved line belongs to God." Some

professors and critics thought his style was eccentric, even insane.
When he graduated from the university, the headmaster said,
"I don't know if we're graduating a genius or a fool!"

Other people thought that Gaudí was brilliant. While working on an exhibit in Paris, Antoni Gaudí met Count Escubí Güell. This was a turning point in Gaudí's life, for Güell immediately saw Gaudí's innate passion and unique vision. Güell became his best friend and sponsor. Gaudí created many hidden treasures, with Güell's support, to illuminate the streets of Barcelona. Gaudí eventually named a park after him.

Then, in 1904, Antoni was asked to redesign the house of a wealthy couple. Inspired by sea coral, Gaudí designed the outside of Casa Batlló with a mosaic made of vibrant colors. He transformed the interior into a masterful work of art combining color, shape, and light. He also built other houses; Casa Mila, covered with a wavy designed facade, and Casa Vicens, with its curvy rooftop mazes, were two of his next projects.

When Güell asked Antoni to design some apartments in a park sitting high above Barcelona, Gaudí began work immediately and moved into a house on-site to immerse himself in the park. Antoni Gaudí saw beauty in broken things. He smashed up plates and glued the shattered pieces together. The sale of the residential complexes proved difficult so, in the end, a public park with majestic views of Barcelona was created: Park Güell.

Smooth tiles with rough edges glistened in the sun, curving as far as the eye could see to make his famous "teacup benches."

The bottoms of glass bottles were set into his ingenious invention. There was perfection in imperfection. Trencadis, or mosaics made of small tiles, covered the rooftops and railings of Parque Güell. Gaudí's art and architecture leaned and curved, bent and contorted. People came from all over the world to see his creations. Some were in awe of his modern innovations: "How marvelous!" Others balked, asking, "¿Está loco?" or "Is this guy crazy?"

Antoni fell ill shortly after completing the park. He came down with Maltese fever and almost died. He even made out his will.

Luckily, he got better and told Güell that he would like to honor God through his work. "Splendid idea," said Güell. "Why don't you build a magnificent cathedral?" Gaudí named the church La Sagrada Familia, or the Sacred Family Cathedral. Gaudí spent the rest of his life working on La Sagrada Familia. He built tall turrets with spiraling staircases just like the conch shells he'd once examined as a boy. Gigantic gargoyles, reminiscent of the animals Gaudí observed on his

long walks and rides in the countryside, guard the cathedral. Curved archways lace the edifice of La Sagrada Familia.

Gaudí said, "Man does not create . . . he discovers." Antoni continued to discover how La Sagrada Familia would bedazzle churchgoers. Even though he was an architect, he had no written plans for the completion of the grandiose cathedral.

Gaudí became so obsessed with making the cathedral, he moved onto the church grounds and lived in a makeshift shack. When a friend asked him, "How can you live so alone?" Gaudí replied, "I am not alone; I am surrounded by an endless array of marvels."

To this day, La Sagrada Familia is still under construction. Nobody knows how to complete it since Gaudí did not leave any drawings. There is much debate about how to finish this towering cathedral in Gaudí's unique style, but architects continue to build twisting staircases, rambling pathways, and winding balconies.

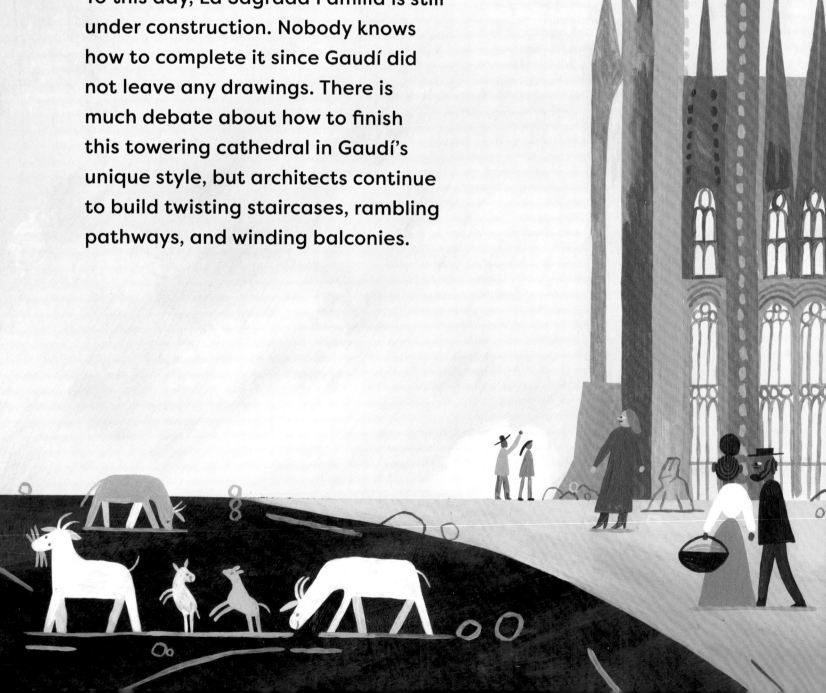

PARK GÜELL

TORRE BELLESGUARD

CASA VICENS

COLEGIO TERESIANO

LA

LA PEDRERA - CASA MILÀ

CASA CALVE

ASA BATLLÓ

Antoni Gaudí changed the face of architecture and art in Barcelona. All over the city are his sparkling, colorful mosaics, illuminating the streets, leading up and down Las Ramblas, and stretching high up into the hills above Barcelona. This book honors the memory and masterpieces of Antoni Gaudí, a visionary before his time.

ANTONI GAUDÍ I CORNET (1852-1926), widely known as Antoni Gaudí in Catalan (Antonio Gaudí in Spanish), was born in Reus, Spain, not far from Barcelona, in the Catalonia region. A gifted architect and artist, Gaudí had great technical skills but was also a very gentle and collaborative leader who built very good relationships. He worked with a team of diverse tradesmen to create every project.

Many of his masterpieces are buildings and parks that fill the streets of Barcelona. Gaudí's works are visited by millions of tourists each year and studied by architects worldwide. Some of his famous creations include:

· La Sagrada Familia Cathedral
· Casa Milà
· Casa Vicens
· Casa Batlló
· Parque Güell

To this day, Gaudi's La Sagrada Familia (the Sacred Family) Cathedral is the most visited monument in all of Spain, but because he didn't leave any plans, La Sagrada Familia is constantly under construction. Many Catalonian people believe that it will never truly be finished since nobody knows exactly how Gaudí wanted it to be.

Text copyright © 2022 by Susan B. Katz
Illustrations copyright © 2022 by Linda Schwalbe
First published in the United States, Great Britain,
Canada, Australia, and New Zealand in 2022 by
NorthSouth Books, Inc., an imprint of NordSüd
Verlag AG, CH-8050 Zürich, Switzerland.

All rights reserved.
No part of this book may be reproduced or
utilized in any form or by any means, electronic or
mechanical, including photocopying, recording,
or any information storage and retrieval system,
without permission in writing from the publisher.

Distributed in the United States by NorthSouth
Books Inc., New York 10016.
Library of Congress Cataloging-in-Publication
Data is available.
ISBN: 978-0-7358-4487-2
1 3 5 7 9 • 10 8 6 4 2
www.northsouth.com

Climate neutral
Print product
ClimatePartner.com/17658-2110-1001